Human Forest

Human Forest

—

Denise Newman

Apogee Press
Berkeley · California
2000

gift 8/07

For Steven,
and for my family

The author is grateful to the editors of the following journals in which some of the poems in this book were first published:

apex of the M: "Human Forest"
Five Fingers Review: "Two Fold"
How2: "Disaster Services"
Mirage #4 PERIOD(ICAL) excerpt from, "Of Later Things Yet to Happen"
Volt: "Anyway the Cows," and an excerpt from, "Of Later Things Yet to Happen"
Why Pear? was first published as a letterpress chapbook by Em Press, and *Of Later Things Yet to Happen* was first published as a Meow Press chapbook.

Thanks to: Bjarne Funch, Eléna Rivera, The Salon, and The Djerassi Resident Artist Program; each helped make this work possible.

Book design by Philip Krayna.

Cover image: "Spacemen" by Helle Frøsig.

ISBN 0-9669937-2-1. Library of Congress Catalog Card Number 99-075476.

Published by Apogee Press, Post Office Box 8177, Berkeley CA, 94707-8177.

Table of Contents

The Pact : 11

Human Forest : 12

Two Fold : 19

Of Later Things Yet to Happen : 21

Now : 46

Many Alone : 47

Why Pear? : 48

Glass : 58

Vast Blue Yawn : 59

Disaster Services : 63

Missed : 66

Some Extra Thing : 67

Two Minds : 68

Trees of Thee : 69

Anyway the Cows : 70

DANTE: "Master, what is this city?"
VIRGIL: "You are still too far back in the dark
to make out what you think you see..."

—*The Divine Comedy* (Inferno, Canto 31)

The Pact

Mind of the forest covered in snow
Sleep being the only private act
Meeting in a sort of sleep at the amber depths
drenched in it
bodies know better
trees are flesh and not spirit

Human Forest

Wind under the dark
sky tosses disposition about
"I'm sorry" shadows
bough bent back
to breaking
Not aiming for bliss
needing only
the good fit

Tell us please, what is personal?

. . .

Filling in sky with meaning
"There'll be hell to pay"
We who make our
own stories
must control
them he says
rolling shape over

Girls wipe themselves
arched over holes
wiping
front to back
as if petting mice
There's an old
saying in America
    What a steal!

. . .

Ache tightens
over dark earth
laid shut
Relax…
the traveler
brings only good things.
But is there help for one
in someone else's longing?

Shape pressing
dead leaves legs
splayed like twigs
face down thinking—
there is no
face on it

. . .

It's what lies concealed
that makes commerce erotic
Slipping into liquid green
youths learn of time
as something passing
Bidders call from the shore:
Come on,
show us what you're worth

Darker than violet
taut shape bouncing
pushing it in mouth
suggested
a night lapped round
by promise

. . .

Leaf buds
extended on thin necks
to mirrors
asking: How will we
know when it's love?
        Girls are already beyond knowing
No natural rutting
season to speak of

Story asks
do you like it?
Wanting a good deal
all around not possible
Little hole ripping in grass
really... I do really... love you

We have to make shapes
for their contradictions

. . .

Ache loosens
off its hinges
spreads a moist
forest floor
this parting wants
another perspective

sometimes empty
is enough

Travelers who
pay for experience
are leaves gathered in
mounds and burned...
To cherish above all
images that
devour

. . .

Were I actually
hungry I would
never tell you
she says with
the "so there" lilt
of the already
captured

Broken off, alone as
an odd fragment
lacking its own function
their words are fragile
dots drawn in
between stars

Please, don't take it personally

. . .

Fingers of light shoot
down between pines
prying forest open
   "scene of crime"
some shapes crouched under
sky gray torment

To sell a life cheap
as was sold to promise

Two Fold

At one time it grew to be one only out of many;
at another, it divided up to be many instead of one.
—Empedocles

1.
crack in the hill tall trees between in a line the crack a lie is
drawn is fertile water runs, not much—between—attend the
once pristine cracked too mud, much I mean ran down after
hill fell bearing cracks in the back will fill with dirt is said
        bury the cracks some mouth had spoken deed tree
bones branch out the wreck in a fingersnap regrets alight
made old the wince a crack gone deep
...how closed I've been

limbs pull back into selves are separate: branch—wing—
thighs of crack—deer limbs—mine—appendices of thought
lead back to centers owned with names in times of strife

pinched in a hinge of I'm and sorry—one alone to night
lamenting all it lost
life cracked meaning from word—
        "I shall be day after next"
limply striving
lie your head back in the warm mud
and wiggle your wormy lips as if...

2.
as if worm and man were one?

lips open and close in rhythm with ocean, saying
    there is no deep beyond
light falls on all it can—hide, then long
for what you hid from by day
deer eating the green cover off
hills turn liquid, groins fill, flowers sink
body of water continuously expanding for fish
is the fits-all world without limbs

Of Later Things Yet to Happen

Morning with its future nature in unfirm pinks of babyhood
anticipation of first step/words, shapeless drips... into first
sin, bringing on afternoon's interrogative light/Miles of
open guilt in saturated haze color of despair... we work or
sleep to shutter the unbearable accusations but never will
relief come feeling/clay oven returning brown just-baked
smell/Licks its genitals after a long sleep is hungry/Behold...
all flesh corrupted is seeking dark red, surfaces absorb
and congeal... Earth is a gentle panting thing to eat but its
blood as darkness overwhelming their throats lie down to
survive/maroon stained glass with bits of pink for eyes
and sexual parts/who haunts changing/and they complain:
can nothing handed down save us

5 a.m.
Fish, fowl, human, mushroom
all gilled and seeking—

6 a.m.
Beneath apparent life sought fish oblivion muck bottom
sinking in it
                    girl who swims well swims down/inhales
forgets her who was instructed with the imperative gesture
(that barreling one with iron breast)

Quietly holes fill with lake... *Let her who desires take the*
water of life without price

7 a.m.
Wise mother of the never naked kind bending in a morning
pool of light to feed her pupa / fingers squeezing in the cream
sauce slimy chunks of fish with softened bones are edible as
eyeballs and mind—
                    Mine, I will churn you through me
thirteen feet of intestines like a Biblical serpent speaking:
        Did Mother say you should seek to know yourself?
No one but a possession—a defenseless Pacific island born
of a volcano…
Eat!
But I am weak for you

8 a.m.

Air is watery in this underground chamber where she makes
her way from the Middle Ages to an aperitif by the stream
they say of St. John's wort

Dreams the knight leaping to rescue trips because it's her
night alone to struggle free from

He crosses a city street holding a day lily sign for her who
is traveling
      the need to know names, all the weeds ever
over-looked, record and read them in the book

9 a.m.
Anywhere along this A–B line may be another way, fallacy

Driving family sees the lit up "Marcal Paper Products"
sign and the question "would this be stationary or some
kind of picnic-ware products" each in them cued/Erotic
thought also driven (lure of night woods) to have narrowly
escaped feeling

Eyes look out the window and see eyes

He warns: Lick life gently behind its ear so as not to be noticed
She inserts her tongue in his and blows

10 a.m.

Human body being of upper half water is unsure of how
to relate to others of the same meandering way

Whencesoever said for the delight of it like drawing in the
lovers who were no one then

Inconsonant as a girl at the end of the 20th century saying
whencesoever to a mirror and winking

Through one image to another... joined like heaven to a
painting of dahlias

Here and there is born a Saint Teresa, foundress of nothing

As if to evaporate rubies into chaos?

Life being a daisy doodle using the hole of loose-leaf paper
for a center

11 a.m.
Keep the wound open until end...

A worn intimacy found among refuse/flies gather at the
crotch where they smell her blood/black meaty winged ones
smashed between hand and thighs

Wound is the nerve of the belief
that destroys the illusion

perpetual sacrifice
in the name of knowing

12 p.m.
Ghetto maze of a story invented with the first word's
idea—Beneath
        as in foundation: *in the end all things will be justified...*
not out or bottom but has another, problem

You see lines are not horizontal but lead the eye down on
a switch-back descent of unraveling/ backward count after
mastering all the numbers forward so positively

        Couldn't we go on climbing into infinity like lambs
quaintly passing time?

Unlambly one you were sinking from the start, remember?
Your zero will be on the underside of meaning order if
you continue rather than stopping for tea and that pity me
small talk

1 p.m.
Out there the calm surface of water... in her the murky below
If only I had days to stare at this lake, she thinks staring
at this lake for days

I mean if only I were this whole lake myself staring—then
what?

The child's erupted skin who down there dwelling in a thought
source of putrefied bodies (leave a devil unchecked he'll roast
and devour whole)

What human way is there of lake wound open and not sick?
Water can lull a rock / No, water and rock lull me... What I want,
water-rock-me lulling all the rest

And in the background
lovers drift by in an open boat and are painted

2 p.m.
Holding a jewel out to her hers already—
his other hand open to receive

Something inward
can be recognized out there
in miniature

Floating nipple held
up to lips suggested
red oval pillow flat against
the flat lovers

Water being the upper half

Reaching for it out there
mistaking it for now, then

3 p.m.
Not the crowd but its shadow/feeling around
the blind shape—words—in whose opinion?

Light-saturated memory straining to see
    I was expecting a public office with paid vacations
    now they say I must go back around the other way
    Only a begging bowl to my name...

All else turns on as a pivot
    You were once the model of satisfaction
Yes glued together moment turning bowl

    Now work a miracle of faith for these thieves
If only they wouldn't admire me for it

4 p.m.
Her private confession in the throng shadowed safely
graceful curve city street simple as one sheet depends on
no special needs
              going along lower water half upper air
between black cliffs mists emptied the little crime its
might/provided for that grayed over the great winnowing
nothing of throng being itself natural/moving sheet of
all crimes bounced slightly forward such that air displaced
is cooling gray pastoral misty lamb scene
simply   must be a Throng Demonstration Day
great zero at sunset waiting in a long line for a free sample
thinking when the end of the world comes—Oh Boy!

5 p.m.
Why art thou not bold and free lines of nodding words tied
together/ their private erotic intent canceled only those without
hope have desire/pigeon hops on its neighbortail wanting to
though unsure—Is it allowed to be sexual in the street?

Planning to say spontaneously: Truly I am moved! and faints

Limp necked words wait for curtain to lift
Do you like—
Oh yes, but actually I like
better, don't you
Certainly, but what's really best
liked and is actually nicest
Oh yes, I couldn't agree with you...

                    As for scenery 365 concealed erotic
                    smiles tied to fishing poles

6 p.m.
Glued bowl moment turning to enter the bus will die
shortly confidence/avoiding looking at damp earth beaded
grass blades smells like myself playing barefoot once

summertime-down-south desire for it opening fly wing
and simultaneously (lines of words can't match this)
other wing suicidal folding in the north

Similar to recognizing someone, going forward is it—
something unfamiliar spreads over the friend/Stranger's
face becomes its insignificant own meanwhile wondering
how so and so is...

Idea-based alluding to smells like reminds me of sort of
dreamed life as in a film almost

7 p.m.
Cultivated desired thing efulges as though cut from a
divine bolt

    freshly invented pleasure smack of no relative but
hers—girl being transported across night or whoever
should be thanked for this life rounded out seed/floating
behind lids just as a sharp tooth forms to press out the
milky one

All potential has its erotic push
bound to it—blood yolk
with an ocean source

8 p.m.
If only we had moments between moments to choose them
she says rubbing on lips red blindly before the show

Moments carrying away moments is destiny at work

Just look inside any idea and you'll find a form

And inside any form an ideal...

Tale must then be the backward stepping motion of truth

Anyway, I wish they'd leave the house lights down
so we could creep out intact

9 p.m.
Hands arranging it is dark, dense
feeling around... smooth stones
damp fur rocks and iron scent...

As the story goes:
Drawn there over fatal waters in someone else's boat,
hero alone reaches the shore on a wreck's fragment/Two
glittering beasts lead the way to the point... Fata, lightly
attired one at the margin of stream/Off falls his armor,
memory, wants only to sigh forever at her feet...

10 p.m.
One part want/one part memory
all of it a loan

Her desire ingests the image
where it once was so complete

She rises to meet him whom she invents
rises with rehearsed graciousness
crosses the imaginary stream

I'm writing you into the poem and it's
not even you so don't be afraid

Who am I then he asks
as though he'd recognize himself

11 p.m.
Questions dead-end as the couple does
                    in a falling-down abandoned castle
This'll do for now she says like the ramshackle answer
                    "who knows"
Beneath the dungeon another, and another again
having forgotten previous manifestations hero feels at home
opens his suitcase and finds her there, moth where
there were his qualities—
not poverty, because more than anything... What?
    wavering, his toe in the cold black pool of her eye
feeling motion though the impulse causes no action
    I...
        forget

12 a.m.

Reclining in dark pools of various reactions/eyes saying
one thing (never has a combination been so satisfying)
and lips: I'm afraid. Afraid. Why are you doing this to me?

She smiles at his belly up too comfortable to do more
than whimper regret not yet seeing herself as a limbless
bolus of sucking gestures—attached as they are at these
points sinking further out of light/Confuse the form and
enter the subtle motion of some third thing becoming at
the edge of sight

imprecisely that which the two would be... rolling sea
water without ruptures such as inquiry...

1 a.m.
Not the "dead floor of Hell" catching corpses as they fall
nor dirt at the end of shovel squirming worm things/but
tamped earth rubbed red by soles and shiny as chestnut
To return to after idea lets go

I only pretended to climax when I did she says
as though just now introducing herself

And all along I envied your pleasure, he tells her

See then how we resemble each other?

Moving deeper into debt with reader she fears there'll have to
be some kind of justification explosion to get out

2 a.m.

Once is now too she says to assure them amidst the peril
of ordinary living
    and so will when be someday today
What I mean is the Ancient Past and Modern Day idea is
lacking...
    If the whole world stood on their roofs at a designated
hour dove off

Always there'd be someone who wouldn't—his word for
hers like aiding the other in to fall/hunter and hunted
trading coats every hundred feet or so until they both must
die or together live

3 a.m.
No narrative without the words they ask "how was your day"
to make actual
Awful, swabs stuffed in bloody holes left to rot
mostly his fault, hers
    Reaching for it, other side
as a sort of fleeing now not possible
Mud and water rising under flapping mouths on stilts
YOU-YOU-ALWAYS-IF-IT-WEREN'T-FOR... repetitive
splash against hull / only hull wearing dumbly
We know how to give up our entire life day after day
and the opposite? would be a meeting a moment
    Do you know what you're saying... I mean *really* know?
our sinking skinsacks in waste mixed with appetite
    Now that decay has advanced it's obvious
only ever needed a little intimacy
in the unraveling

4 a.m.
Time let us rest
Bodies stretched out as death-like sentences—
allusion to *the spirit of man is dreaming*
Breath pedals backward / forward-moving wake
every gesture collected every trick never plural
floats the surface like dead fish
Who is awake to feel alarm...
Are you on time yet?

Now

the mind turns backward

recalls a sea

the body rests in its cave

and the sea goes nowhere

Many Alone

A thought is not thinking
"What's going on in there?"
Turns away… "oh nothing"
hidden, like spots on a mattress
the old roll over
          "I figured it out and it's all your fault"
bubble releasing from foam on wave—
its fragile wobble upward
—won't get far alone,
collapses
          "I'm so lonely" heap says
wetting the thought down thoroughly
as though washing
ceremonial cloths
Crowd wrapped in feeling
all alone and special—
the five o'clock push
thought: *if only these others*
weren't here crossing minds
like sour sewer air blown up
from underground trains
Each having had a day
empties pockets on the nightstand
          "Fine, and yours?"

Why Pear?

Dionysus in a boat
on a plate
chipped and cracked...

As is, I'd been saying
as is, is as, as is

    No warranty

Seeing him as a word
that describes, it is said
  He is fake
he is to be that
our wish to participate

the magic world

Camouflaged as a person, anyone
    moving so as not to be found—
voided
Habits of being
comfortable sightseeing
    …said
    give us that perfectly
eluding all and earth bird
talent

Where a word lifts up then said
I am not
    carried beyond and read
    cold, very cold, like the pencil she holds...
—write that down

propelled by vague
forgot, is feeling

why passion, why pear
Twice-born god

Carrying the bodies across fields
in love with the body
carrying too late

play that back again

Golden Age greeting
of sand-glued petal wings
broken apart with tongue

—fortune
read out of sequence
too soon

Dressing
this wait
  what's a window—
which side?
peering between
in there first ice
thin meaning

Now is a place
  complete transparency

Eat the pear, he says

  to divide?

No, devour

Surface as absolute limit
of inside, lacking
    what follows words I want...

Skins touch passing
human forest

If object were complete
never a need of assurance

    Are we almost there?

This wine illusion of oneness
tongued to death
they say
your infallible weapon was madness
     Too kind, all of you—
softly falling bodies
from a high-rise window
in a moment
become word—

Year of the Was

Papa? Was ist das?
    Eine kleine Fremde

Licking around outside
the bloody sack wants in—
Tell me
    I'm not a stranger I'm a person, right?

People always passing far too many
indefinite relative
who

You could be a star
You could be someone—

Nearing/distance
person having nothing to do with place
drawn "in his arms"
    with a sinking gesture

Give me a name
You mean, oblivion?

already out in the big sky travelers
are floating lights
each with a window asking
    is this it?
Can't say it all place of meeting
A Greek god tourist in photocopied love time
written in the passing...
      "but they look so real"

Glass

Had I understood it my life would've expressed it
not the poem
Or is the overflowing of a poem just that?

Paling sea at dusk—its surface throbs a little
she says, my paintings should not be comfortably full
but like a glass almost overflowing with water

A tug at my attention makes me turn
before knowing what it is I ought to be doing
instead of this washed stillness observing curl of
clear on dark blue wave unrolling with no tidy purpose

Bouncing off scene—panicked over
I'm as transparent as water

Vast Blue Yawn

pale moon, thumbs inside waistband hoists trunks up,
as though dead, towel over arm, looks down at wife
who lifts arm slowly dries under and around, also dead
to him. can see breast what sticks out from her big back.
dream-like. evading despair one joins the dead. wobbly
getting feet into little holes of underwear, thinking, they
are not me, in my view, and yet—

the great sea-eraser

moves feet looks at wife goes toward her looking away,
was? she says. one dies one after another (eyes first) girl
walks by cup of seawater extended talking to herself.
goes to mom who bends exposing bare white bottom
smells cup offered. I did this once, thinks mother? girl
runs off. going back after reason to be there has died.
beached shell bleached out from sand seen.

Do you find that attractive?—
(referring to the naked man on shore) I'm not aroused
if that's what you mean. no? — swims off. clear in his
mind. no going back. swims toward light becomes it,
who was once me or more me, or maybe — made me be
more fully myself including him too as me. now what?

tired shadow
      spreading
spared nothing

dog rolling in the rotten fish smell. two fingers go up
slip suit down over rump. returning to a dead place, like
looking at food in the market not reminded of cooking
or eating. just shapes. all of it of one piece and this extra
thing—(me). boy throws towel over shoulders runs
shouting *I am superman!* Did you have any hope? No.
I did.

gesture of one arm across big breasts other elbow resting
in hand, hand cradles chin. not thinking or waiting. she's
dead or just imitating plants in the sea as we began,
surfacely. writing is dreaming until one puts it all together.
little rowboat light water whitens. so who am I without
him I wrote—a blank sea face when one looks directly.

holds sides stomach out looking down at wife, rubs
backside, enters blue, rubs stomach, looks back at wife
open-mouthed. immeasurable dark face east. writing it
like scratching.

somehow it doesn't
connect—
        ("that's her problem")
day after day
blanksea face—
        it just goes on
mimicking itself

moving toward familiarity (dead) not seeing, rupturing to
see again. no easy exit from despair. man lightly wiggles
shorts come down nakedly into water swinging arms.
quiet ease absence of volition. girl slips glasses into
pocket goes toward blue turns with hands on shoulders
to mother who's standing there like a stump. man leaves
sea head cocked wiggling finger in ear, looks at me, at
shoulder, scratches.

rolling around in putrid end. making a living of it, like
mistaking the shadow for the gull seen sideways—the
infinite consistency of self, exhausted
dead wave pretend end in other.

tall lean man leaning naked and reading, no tan lines
it just goes on

accidental shapes against the blue yawn. big belly makes
genitals tiny rubbing hand towel up inside leg, then the
other. stands staring as though a plant. we rarely know it
is going on it just goes on like dreams. sky and sea blue-
makers. meaning constantly needs being invented.

kissed his lips fall off for dead.
—he means it.

what's observed untroubled as sea is quietly blue. holding
the big stick dog leaping up barking head off, goes in
in graceful leaps. gull flapping flies up and down as
through a hilly sky. couple throws under-handed colorful
balls. without a moral. three kids digging by shore.

Disaster Services

1.

The never sleeping worm
threads rot with all the living,
(no use in charming the little bugger once it's bitten)
The woman sniffs and wonders
what the apple thinks of her

2.

All flesh is edible
smiling like a bite
in an apple going brown
    Well how do I look?
The white-gloved glass handlers
holding her pretty up could
slip threat sunk up to
lips in chat

3.

Lure of words
on lines
talks him to her, doing it as her bit
Come tangle your long ruinous arms
with mine dear—

4.
Coupling like scaffolded scaffolding
in their guts—what?
a hollow gassy feel—*Sweet me up Daddy,*
    don't stop!

5.
Inserts his in her, on sale
is moral to save and amass
Well done honey glow
he's a family man now
Whose worm rules?

6.
Fall little apple fall
far far from the tree
their teeth stuck out of their mouths
at baby smiling back so prettily
Good serves girl deserves better
Go ahead, ravish my youth if you must

7.
Edible host family eating toast and jam famished
morning newspaper around disasters
and Mom's assuring humming them
that nothing's going on in there—
happiest make believe bosom time

8.
Dusty moth earthed
swollen legs up dreamed
magazine unblemished life
flipping through "someday" vague sum
—all over the neighborhood
trees bow down and raise up
in penance for them

9.
Holes in Sunday, in the clothed and flaccid flesh
Father with his head
sunk back into cushions
looking upward as if at birds
carrying off chunks
of him

10.
They bought a fraud
"Oh well" Mom says
what can be said
with a devouring emptiness
about the head?
This isn't it at all

Missed

tangle of grasses and thistle mist pushed down in fits
and knots like hair slept wet a web across the face of night
unrest is no ideal or garden-order—one thinks of death and
panics

      a fly on the end of nerves in fog-filtered light for
days like an ache in the brain that throbs with the word
"more" or "better"
Can life itself be lacking?

      leaves of nettle an arrangement of hooks
that catch the soles of flesh step lightly over one feels
one's safe—I'm fine, I'm feathered—to make a home
on the brow and not look down

comb the lawn alone each every greedy dawn
and preen just right just so—
then in the evening comb it back
the other way to vary

she thinks of life as licked
but often sighs

there's eternity in order
and boredom

Some Extra Thing

The red floppy bow bouncing on the back of a head
    down Market St.
Bows are an extra thing like circles around numbers or
    worse, half circles.
Like "you know" and "like"
Who is grabbing for the box of individually wrapped
    butter bricks?
The transparent man needs to be decked out to be seen.
What if every wisp of nature, each rock, dandelion, oak
were dressed? as though it were—
our saying: igneous, weed, live oak...
never perceiving the invisible body bowing against sky
our having become like tax and gratuities not included
the waitress underlines her name on the check swerving
the line downward and crossing it with two short lines.
Tiny little. A fence around a tree.
He finishes the cough off with another... Excuse me?
I said, would you like some less?
Oh it's too late for that but thank you anyway
and bends tying double bows,
there now.

Two Minds

Let girls have puppies and pink, let boys say fart and
  break things
I must be getting older, better proportioned to the ways
  of the world
I'll fax you, sure, or email me... either way we'll connect...
voice dropping off weary cliff...
too much undone too far until —
a nuthatch running upside down the tree doesn't feel
slow to watch as does a computer booting up hurts
Bird says, relax nothing'll work out anyway
Machine says, if only you worked a little harder you might
just get somewhere
Double-minded, twin-eyed under a cleaved sky heaving
How might I live?
Man in my bed me out with the birds writing: I wish to
  be in bed
Skin wants this too. We are agreed. Too attached to syntax
and gushy comfort

Trees of Thee

Trees have names
and streets have tree names
My feet are hot in English America
Elmwood Ave, a Helmsley Palace polished
The beeches in Poland do not end,
as Milosz said, there. They are in
Glottal Stop Denmark too
where wood is called tree too
In May the airy leaf-light softens
their voices as they go dressed in it
kissing under sea-green cover saying "Steven"
—surprised loved has a name too
apart from ours Honey

Any Way the Cows

They want love like mad
this madness' divine steeple top
in silver air and they'd all
be giddy kissing each other
when someone much older
walks in and says,
"You drunken fools!"

What sprung loose need not
be mended. It had got late.
so? It will
got late again. And all
the bells at once reminding

no-thing-do-it-no-thing-do-it-no-

The great peopled-over world
and the little ephipanies popping
through like holes in the all-weather
plastic sky covering

"really, we just want to be ourselves"

pancakes and elastic waistbands
we're not ashamed of our humanness
said collectively from TV: "It's your world,
you can do what you want"

I want to kiss the old farts and catch them
whence they fall off their platformed feet.
I want to feed everyone in the wide world
the laxative word relax.
I want plenty of room for all the I's and we's
hammered into position by weather.

The cows' waddle and push
up the steeple hillside at sunset
the sighing lovers follow while
the others groan, "how corny"
Any way is a way
honey—
just jump

PHOTO: Butch Baluyut

DENISE NEWMAN is a poet and teacher living in San Francisco. Her translation of *The Painted Room* by the Danish poet Inger Christensen is published by The Harvill Press, U.K. Her work has appeared in *Volt, Talisman, Chain,* and *Five Fingers Review,* where she is a general editor.